THIS BOOK
SCRATCHES!

SARAH MACHAJEWSKI

Gareth Stevens
PUBLISHING

Please visit our website, www.garethstevens.com. For a free color catalog of all our high-quality books, call toll free 1-800-542-2595 or fax 1-877-542-2596.

Cataloging-in-Publication Data

Names: Machajewski, Sarah.
Title: This book scratches! / Sarah Machajewski.
Description: New York : Gareth Stevens Publishing, 2020. | Series: Beastly books for the brave | Includes glossary and index.
Identifiers: ISBN 9781538233672 (pbk.) | ISBN 9781538233696 (library bound) | ISBN 9781538233689 (6pack)
Subjects: LCSH: Claws--Juvenile literature. | Animals--Adaptation--Juvenile literature. | Animal defenses--Juvenile literature.
Classification: LCC QL942.M33 2020 | DDC 591.47'9--dc23

First Edition

Published in 2020 by
Gareth Stevens Publishing
111 East 14th Street, Suite 349
New York, NY 10003

Copyright © 2020 Gareth Stevens Publishing

Designer: Katelyn E. Reynolds
Editor: Kate Light

Photo credits: Cover, p. 1 (claws) michal.varga/Shutterstock.com; cover, pp. 1-24 (book cover) Ensuper/Shutterstock.com; cover, p. 1-24 (tape) Picsfive/Shutterstock.com; cover, pp. 1-24 (decorative elements) cute vector art/Shutterstock.com; cover, pp. 1-24 (book interior and wood background) robert_s/Shutterstock.com; pp. 4-21 (fun fact background) Miloje/Shutterstock.com; p. 5 (reptiles) Michael Maes/Shutterstock.com; p. 5 (mammamls) ZARIN ANDREI/Shutterstock.com; p. 5 (birds) Gary C. Tognoni/Shutterstock.com; p. 7 Paul Crum/Science Source/Getty Images; p. 9 (main) Bence Mate/Nature Picture Library/Getty Images; p. 9 (inset) Anna Kucherova/Shutterstock.com; p. 10 Suzi Eszterhas/Minden Pictures/Getty Images; p. 11 Konstantin Tronin/Shutterstock.com; p. 13 Laura Duellman/Shutterstock.com; p. 15 Ondrej Prosicky/Shutterstock.com; p. 17 (main) worldswildlifewonders/Shutterstock.com; p. 17 (inset) Auscape/Universal Images Group/Getty Images; p. 18 Jamie osborn/Shutterstock.com; p. 19 Tim Platt/Stone/Getty Images; p. 20 Christophe Courteau/Gamma-Rapho via Getty Images; p. 21 Insights/UIG via Getty Images.

Printed in the United States of America

CPSIA compliance information: Batch #CS19GS: For further information contact Gareth Stevens, New York, New York at 1-800-542-2595.

CONTENTS

WORDS IN THE GLOSSARY APPEAR IN **BOLD** TYPE THE FIRST TIME THEY ARE USED IN THE TEXT.

SWIPE! SCRATCH!

Watch out! The beasts in this book aren't afraid to take a swipe at you! This is a book full of clawed creatures. Are you brave enough to read on?

The animal kingdom is a wild world of animals that share one common goal: survival. **Adaptations** help animals survive in their **environment.** Claws are a terrifying adaptation that help the creatures in this book stay alive. The only question is—will you make it out alive, too?

FACTS FOR THE FEARLESS

THERE'S A CLAWED CREATURE READING THIS BOOK RIGHT NOW—YOU! YOUR FINGERNAILS ARE A TYPE OF CLAW.

TYPES OF ANIMALS WITH CLAWS

BIRDS

MAMMALS

REPTILES

On **BIRDS OF PREY**, like this great horned owl, claws are called talons.

MAMMALS like house cats and big cats have sharp claws!

Alligators have scary claws, but they use them to dig—not to attack!

Watch out! Reptiles, birds, and many kinds of mammals have sharp claws. There are also a few kinds of amphibians that have clawlike structures, though these aren't considered true claws.

CREATIVE CLAWS

Claws are sharp, curved structures that grow out of animals' paws or feet. Animals use their claws in all kinds of useful—and scary—ways.

Some creatures use claws as a form of **defense**. They'll swipe at an enemy with their sharp claws **extended**. Claws can also be used to hunt. Some beasts use their claws to catch, hold onto, or kill their prey. Other animals use their claws to dig! Giant armadillos have huge claws for digging into termite mounds.

FACTS FOR THE FEARLESS

INSTEAD OF ROLLING UP INTO A BALL WHEN THEY'RE SCARED, GIANT ARMADILLOS USE THEIR POWERFUL CLAWS TO DIG HOLES TO HIDE IN.

CLAWS COME IN ALL SHAPES AND SIZES. GIANT ARMADILLOS HAVE HUGE CLAWS COMPARED TO THE SIZE OF THEIR BODY. THEIR BODIES ARE ABOUT 3 FEET (0.9 M) LONG, AND THEIR CLAWS ARE 8 INCHES (20 CM) LONG!

LETHAL LIZARDS

Green basilisks have long, curved claws that help them run quickly across the ground. They can run over 6 miles (10 km) per hour! Like many lizards, green basilisks also use their claws to climb. They spend most of their time in trees, and their claws help them grip the bark.

Other lizards, such as the huge Komodo dragon, use their claws for hunting. Komodo dragons jump on their prey and dig in with their sharp claws.

FACTS FOR THE FEARLESS

KOMODO DRAGONS HAVE POWERFUL CLAWS TO CATCH PREY, BUT THEY KILL WITH A **VENOMOUS** BITE. THE BIG LIZARDS FOLLOW THEIR BITTEN PREY UNTIL IT DIES FROM THE VENOM. THEN THE DRAGONS FEAST!

KOMODO DRAGON

GREEN BASILISKS HAVE SPECIAL FLAPS OF SKIN ON THEIR FEET THAT HELP THEM RUN ACROSS WATER!

KILLER CAT CLAWS

The world's big cats, such as lions and tigers, have **fierce** claws that can scratch you to pieces. They use their claws for **protection** and hunting.

Cats have retractable claws, which means they're hidden inside the paw when not in use. When a big cat is ready to attack, it extends its long, sharp claws.

Cheetahs are the only cats with claws that don't fully retract. They need their claws out to help them grip the ground as they run at high speeds!

CHEETAH CLAWS

JUST LIKE HOUSE CATS, BIG CATS SCRATCH THEIR CLAWS ON OBJECTS TO KEEP THEM SHARP AND CLEAN.

BEASTLY BEARS

Among the world's biggest animals are bears—large, furry mammals with tons of power and equally sharp claws. Bear claws aren't as curved as cat claws. This helps bears dig in the ground for food, such as roots, nuts, and even small animals.

Some bears use their claws to climb. Black bears are very good climbers! When threatened, they'll climb to safety. Black bears also use their claws to mark trees with scratches. This is their way of leaving messages to other bears in the area!

GRIZZLY BEAR CLAWS, PICTURED HERE, ARE MUCH LONGER THAN BLACK BEAR CLAWS. THEY CAN BE UP TO 4 INCHES (10.2 CM) LONG!

WILD WOLVERINES

Are you brave enough to take on an animal with claws and paws as big as these? This wolverine's long, sharp claws will leave a scratch you'll never forget!

Wolverines are powerful creatures. They use their claws for climbing trees, digging dens, and burying food. When they find a meal, wolverines use their claws to dig into their prey. Then, with one strong, sharp bite, wolverines go in for the kill.

FACTS FOR THE FEARLESS

THE SUPERHERO CHARACTER WOLVERINE HAS LONG, SHARP CLAWS AND IS NAMED AFTER THE FEARSOME WILD ANIMAL!

WOLVERINES SORT OF LOOK LIKE BEARS, BUT THEY'RE ACTUALLY PART OF THE WEASEL FAMILY.

15

THE PECULIAR PLATYPUS

What is this strange animal? It's a platypus, and it's just as **unique** as it looks. It has adaptations that help it live in water and on land. It also has some sharp structures that help it survive.

Platypuses have webbed feet with claws. When platypuses are on land, they use their claws to help them grip the ground as they run. What's really wild is that male platypuses have a sharp spur on each of their back feet. They use these spurs to pierce their enemies during fights!

FACTS FOR THE FEARLESS

PLATYPUSES RELEASE VENOM THROUGH THEIR SPURS.

PLATYPUS FOOT WITH SPUR

THE PLATYPUS'S SHARP SPURS ARE NOT AT ALL LIKE THE CLAWS FOUND ON A LION OR BEAR. HOWEVER, THEY'RE SIMILAR IN THAT THEY HELP PLATYPUSES SURVIVE ATTACKS FROM ENEMIES.

THE TRUTH ABOUT TALONS

Some of the sharpest claws belong to birds of prey. These fearsome, feathered beasts include eagles, owls, and falcons. Their large, curved claws are also known as talons. One brush with talons can mean certain death. They're sharp enough to pierce through skin and strong enough to tear apart flesh.

Birds of prey don't use their claws for scratching like other animals. Talons are used for capturing and killing prey. In the wild world of clawed beasts, it's the strongest—and sharpest—who survive!

BALD EAGLE TALONS

EAGLES HAVE FOUR TALONS. SMALL PREY HAVE NO CHANCE OF ESCAPING THE EAGLE'S TIGHT GRIP.

19

DIG IN!

You've reached the end of this beastly book! Did you make it through unscratched? Then you're ready to keep exploring fearsome claws on your own.

What interesting beasts will you meet next? The three-toed sloth, whose claws are so long that they make up 17 percent of its body length? Or maybe you'll learn about giant ant eaters, who can fight off jaguars with their huge claws! Wherever you look, there are even more bizarre creatures to discover. Are you ready to dig in?

GIANT ANT EATER

THREE-TOED SLOTHS USE THEIR HUGE CLAWS TO **GRASP** TREE BRANCHES. THEY SLEEP 15 TO 20 HOURS A DAY HIGH UP IN THE TREES.

GLOSSARY

adaptation: a change in a type of animal that makes it better able to live in its surroundings

bird of prey: a bird that hunts and eats other animals

defense: a way of guarding against an enemy

den: a wild animal's hidden home

environment: the conditions that surround a living thing and affect the way it lives

extend: to stretch out

fierce: eager to fight or kill

grasp: to take and hold something

mammal: a warm-blooded animal that has a backbone and hair, breathes air, and feeds milk to its young

protection: the state of being kept from harm

unique: one of a kind

venomous: able to produce a poisonous liquid called venom that is harmful to other animals

FOR MORE INFORMATION

BOOKS

Lindeen, Mary. *Animal Defenses*. Chicago, IL: Norwood House Press, 2018.

Owen, Ruth. *Wings, Paws, Scales, and Claws: Let's Investigate Animal Bodies*. Cornwall, England: Ruby Tuesday Books, 2017.

Spilsbury, Louise, and Richard Spilsbury. *Animal Adaptations*. Minneapolis, MN: Bellwether Media, Inc., 2017.

WEBSITES

The Adaptations of a Lion's Claws
animals.mom.me/adaptations-lions-claws-6442.html
Read all about why lions have claws and how they help this beast survive.

Claws Out: Things You Didn't Know About Claws
thomsonsafaris.com/blog/animal-claws-out/
Visit this website to learn more about claws.

Which Animals Have the Longest Claws?
news.nationalgeographic.com/2015/09/150912-animals-science-largest-claws-talons/
National Geographic takes a look at the longest claws in the animal kingdom.

INDEX